Dear Parent:
Your child's love of reading starts here!

Every child learns to read in a different way and at his or her own speed. Some go back and forth between reading levels and read favorite books again and again. Others read through each level in order. You can help your young reader improve and become more confident by encouraging his or her own interests and abilities. From books your child reads with you to the first books he or she reads alone, there are I Can Read Books for every stage of reading:

SHARED READING
Basic language, word repetition, and whimsical illustrations, ideal for sharing with your emergent reader

BEGINNING READING
Short sentences, familiar words, and simple concepts for children eager to read on their own

READING WITH HELP
Engaging stories, longer sentences, and language play for developing readers

READING ALONE
Complex plots, challenging vocabulary, and high-interest topics for the independent reader

ADVANCED READING
Short paragraphs, chapters, and exciting themes for the perfect bridge to chapter books

I Can Read Books have introduced children to the joy of reading since 1957. Featuring award-winning authors and illustrators and a fabulous cast of beloved characters, I Can Read Books set the standard for beginning readers.

A lifetime of discovery begins with the magical words **"I Can Read!"**

Visit www.icanread.com for information
on enriching your child's reading experience.

P9-CEY-234

I Can Read Book® is a trademark of HarperCollins Publishers.

Danny and the Dinosaur and the New Puppy
Copyright © 2015 by Anti-Defamation League Foundation, Inc., The Authors Guild Foundation, Inc., ORT America, Inc., United Negro College Fund, Inc.
All rights reserved. Manufactured in China.
No part of this book may be used or reproduced in any manner whatsoever without written permission except in the case of brief quotations embodied in critical articles and reviews. For information address HarperCollins Children's Books, a division of HarperCollins Publishers, 195 Broadway, New York, NY 10007.
www.icanread.com

Library of Congress Control Number: 2014956840
ISBN 978-0-06-228153-1 (trade bdg.)—ISBN 978-0-06-228152-4 (pbk.)

David Cutting and Rick Farley used Adobe Photoshop to create the digital illustrations for this book.
Typography by Jeff Shake

15 16 17 18 19   SCP   10 9 8 7 6 5 4 3 2 1   ❖   First Edition

I Can Read!™ BEGINNING READING 1

Syd Hoff's

DANNY AND THE DINOSAUR

and the New Puppy

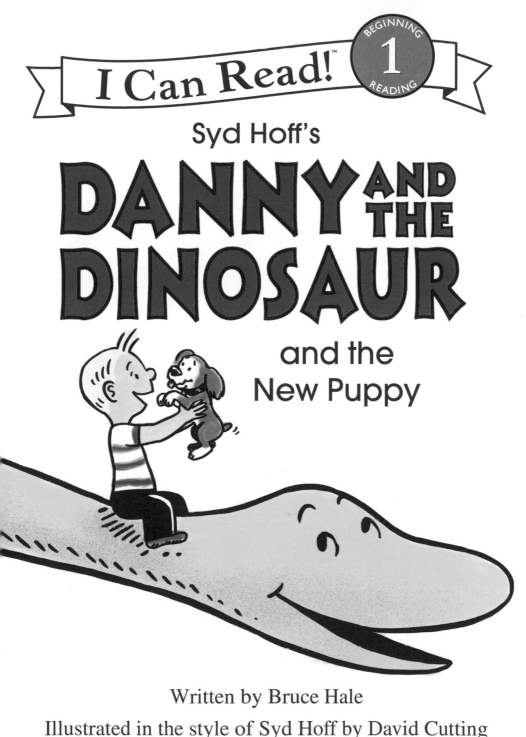

Written by Bruce Hale

Illustrated in the style of Syd Hoff by David Cutting

HARPER

An Imprint of HarperCollinsPublishers

The dinosaur went to the park
to meet his friend Danny.
As he walked up,
he heard Danny say,
"Roll over!"

So the dinosaur rolled over.

THUMP!

"Oops!" said Danny.

"I was talking to my new puppy.

Want to play with us?"

"Let's play!"

said the dinosaur.

Danny threw a stick. "Fetch!"

The puppy came back with the stick.

The dinosaur came back

with a tree.

Danny said, "Sit!"

The puppy sat.

But when the dinosaur sat . . .

CRASH!

He really sat!

"Oops," said the dinosaur.

"I'm proud of you both,"

said Danny.

"Good dog."

He gave the puppy a treat.

"Good dinosaur," said Danny.

He gave the dinosaur lots of treats.

The day was hot.

They went to the pool to cool off.

Splish-splash went the puppy.

SPLISH-SPLASH went the dinosaur.

The friends played at being pirates.

The dinosaur was the pirate ship.

"Ahoy, mateys!" cried Danny.

All the kids climbed on board

while the puppy stood guard.

"Time to dry off," said Danny.

The puppy shook her fur dry.

Shake-shake-shake!

But when the dinosaur tried

to dry himself . . .

Shake-shake-*SPLOOSH!*
everybody got wetter.

The sun set. It was getting late.

"Good-bye, dinosaur," said Danny.

"I wish you could come

home with us."

"Good-bye, Danny," said the dinosaur.

"I wish I could come, too."

The sad dinosaur watched them go.

Then the dinosaur trudged back
to the museum all by himself.

"I wish our day didn't have to end,"

said Danny.

But then he smiled.

Danny had an idea. . . .

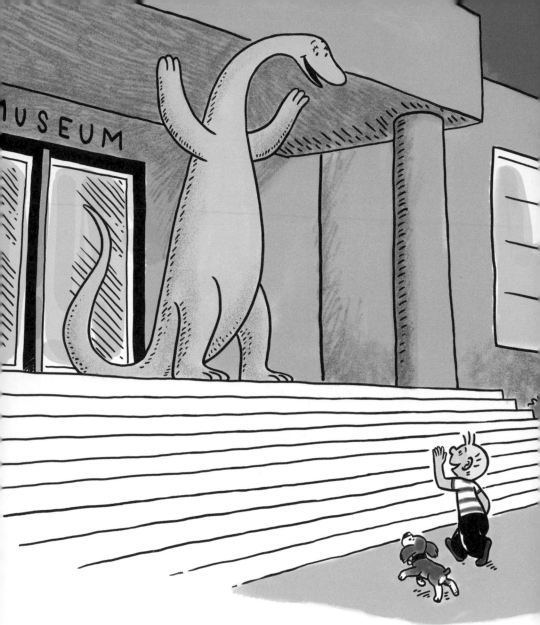

"What are you doing here?"
asked the dinosaur.

"Time for a sleepover!" said Danny.

The friends played some quiet games

and had some snacks.

Then they snuggled up to sleep.

"I love sleepovers," said Danny.

"How about you?"

But the dinosaur said nothing.

The dinosaur was asleep.